I Care About MY FRIENDS

Liz Lennon

I0808740

CRABTREE
PUBLISHING COMPANY
WWW.CRABTREEBOOKS.COM

CRABTREE
PUBLISHING COMPANY
WWW.CRABTREEBOOKS.COM

Published in Canada
Crabtree Publishing
616 Welland Avenue
St. Catharines, ON
L2M 5V6

Published in the United States
Crabtree Publishing
347 Fifth Ave,
Suite 1402-145
New York, NY 10016

Published by Crabtree Publishing Company in 2021

All rights reserved. No part of this publication may be reproduced, stored in a retrieval system or be transmitted in any form or by any means, electronic mechanical, photocopying, recording, or otherwise, without the prior written permission of the copyright owner.

First published in 2020 by The Watts Publishing Group
Copyright © The Watts Publishing Group, 2020

Printed in the U.S.A./122020/CG20201014

Author: Liz Lennon

Editorial director: Kathy Middleton

Editors: Sarah Peutrill, Janine Deschenes

Design: Collaborate

Illustrator: Michael Buxton

Proofreader: Melissa Boyce

Production coordinator & Prepress technician: Samara Parent

Print coordinator: Katherine Berti

Library and Archives Canada Cataloguing in Publication

Title: I care about my friends / Liz Lennon.
Other titles: My friends
Names: Lennon, Liz (Children's non-fiction writer), author. | Buxton, Michael (Artist), illustrator.
Description: Illustrated by Michael Buxton. | Previously published: London: Franklin Watts, 2020. | Includes index.
Identifiers: Canadiana (print) 20200357107 | Canadiana (ebook) 20200357158 | ISBN 9781427128928 (hardcover) | ISBN 9781427128980 (softcover) | ISBN 9781427129048 (HTML)
Subjects: LCSH: Friendship—Juvenile literature.
Classification: LCC BF723.F68 L46 2021 | DDC j177/.62—dc23

Library of Congress Cataloging-in-Publication Data

Names: Lennon, Liz (Children's non-fiction writer), author. | Buxton, Michael (Artist), illustrator.
Title: I care about my friends / Liz Lennon ; illustrated by Michael Buxton.
Other titles: My friends
Description: New York, NY : Crabtree Publishing Company, 2021. | Series: I care about | First published in Great Britain in 2020 by the Watts Publishing Group.
Identifiers: LCCN 2020045676 (print) | LCCN 2020045677 (ebook) | ISBN 9781427128928 (hardcover) | ISBN 9781427128980 (paperback) | ISBN 9781427129048 (ebook)
Subjects: LCSH: Friendship in children--Juvenile literature. | Friendship--Juvenile literature.
Classification: LCC HQ784.F7 L46 2021 (print) | LCC HQ784.F7 (ebook) | DDC 302.34083--dc23
LC record available at https://lccn.loc.gov/2020045676
LC ebook record available at https://lccn.loc.gov/2020045677

Contents

Friendship is fun

Friends are people you enjoy spending time with. You might share the same interests and hobbies. You might like to tell jokes and laugh with your friends. You probably like playing and having fun together!

Friends **support** and care for each other. They are important parts of everyone's lives.

Making friends

How do you choose your friends? Often, we choose friends who have the same interests as us. We also choose friends who make us laugh. Friends should also make each other feel good about themselves.

Everyone is different. Some people like to have many different friends. Other people would rather have one or two very close friends.

Feeling shy

It is not always easy to make new friends. Sometimes, we feel **shy** when we meet others for the first time. It can be especially hard to make new friends when you have moved to a new place and do not know anyone yet. It is normal to feel shy sometimes. Joining clubs or sports teams can help you make friends if you feel shy.

Making new friends is easier when we remember that everyone has the same feelings sometimes.

Try smiling and asking questions.

Say: Hello, what do you like to play?

Say: I like to play soccer and draw pictures. Do you want to play with me?

How should I treat my friends?

A big part of being a friend is treating others with kindness and **respect**. There are many ways to do this. You can take turns when you're playing a game. You can learn to be a good listener. You can tell a joke to cheer up a friend who feels unhappy.

Think about it

- What ways can you be a good friend to others?
- How do you like to be treated by your friends?

Understanding feelings

Learning to understand your friends' feelings is a great way to be a good friend. Ask how a friend is feeling to learn their **point of view**. You can also learn how to understand your own feelings. This will help you **communicate** more clearly and ask for help when you need it.

HAPPY

SAD

CALM

GRUMPY

ANGRY

GRATEFUL

Just like the weather, feelings can come and go. Having different feelings is a normal part of life.

Sharing is caring

Having friends means that sometimes we have to share things. Have you ever shared toys, games, and snacks with your friends? Sometimes sharing is hard! It is important, however, to treat others how you would like to be treated.

Why is sharing important?

When we share with others, we give them part or all of something we have. We should share with others without expecting something in return. Chances are that your friends will share with you as well!

Sharing is an important way to be close to our friends.

Not getting along

Friends do not always get along. It is normal to argue or to feel upset with a friend. Maybe a friend leaves you out of a game, or you can't agree on which game to play.

Remember...

Friends should never ask you to do things you don't want to do.

If this happens, politely say no and walk away. Speak to a trusted adult if you feel worried about it.

When you are not getting along with a friend, it is a good idea to speak to them about how you feel. Try to understand their feelings too.

Making up

If you are not getting along with a friend, talking is the best way to find out what's going on. Imagine how your friend is feeling. That's not easy. You have to put yourself "in their shoes." This means you think about how you would feel if you were in your friend's position.

What should I do?

- Say what you are feeling, but try not to focus only on what you feel your friend did wrong.
- Listen carefully to what your friend has to say.
- If you still can't agree, ask a trusted adult to help. Don't expect them to take sides!

What is bullying?

The best way to treat friends is to be kind. We should never hurt our friends. Bullying is never part of a good friendship. Pushing or hitting, calling someone names, spreading rumors, and leaving someone out of games are all examples of bullying.

One person can be a bully. Groups of people can bully others too. But bullying is not always easy to see. Notice when a friend feels hurt or angry about how they have been treated. Ask questions about how they feel. Show them you care about them.

What if I am being bullied?

- Walk away from the bully or bullies if you can.
- Tell a trusted adult.
- Remind yourself that you are an important person who does not deserve to be treated badly.

Words can hurt

The words we use are important. A lot of bullying comes from words alone. Imagine how you would feel if someone said any of these things to you or about you.

Do your best to think before you speak. Don't say hurtful things to your friends!

You're not my friend.
Don't play with her!
He's acting like a baby.
You're terrible at that!
I don't like you.

Best friends

Some people have a best friend. A best friend might be someone you spend a lot of time with or have a lot in common with. If you have a best friend, that's great. Don't leave out your other friends though. Everyone should feel included. Not everyone has a best friend. Some people have more than one best friend. All kinds of friends are OK.

What if my best friend likes someone else?

Your best friend may want to play with other friends too. Sometimes, this might feel hurtful. If you don't want to join in, that is OK. Your best friend is allowed to have other friends, just as you are.

Friendship groups

Do you have a group of friends you like to spend time with? Groups of friends can be a little like a jigsaw puzzle. Each person is different. Sometimes, they do not fit together. But in time, everyone completes a beautiful puzzle!

Think about it

- What is the main reason you get along with the friends in your group?
- What would you do if one of your friends was unkind to or bullied someone else in the group?

Changing friendships

As you grow, you will meet new friends. You might meet them at a new club or a new school. As your interests change, you might have more in common with new people. It's fun to make new friends.

What if I'm worried about change?

Changing friendships are a normal part of life. If you are sad or worried about changing friendships, talk to a trusted adult about how you are feeling.

You might keep some of your old friends for a long time. But as you change and grow up, you might drift apart from some friends.

Remember...

Smile, ask questions, and try new activities to make friends.

Everyone is different. It is OK to have a few friends or many friends.

Treat your friends with kindness.

Learn to understand your feelings and the feelings of others.

Sharing is caring.

Don't be a bully.

Arguing with friends sometimes is normal.

It is normal for friendships to change.

Words to Know

communicate To share information through talking, writing, body language, and more

point of view A person's perspective, or how they see things

respect Showing that you think someone or something is important

shy Feeling nervous or uncomfortable around others

support To help someone and show you care about their success

Index